More Poetic Meanderings

K Morris

Contents

Acknowledgements

I would like to thank the following:

Dave Higgins for proof reading and formatting my manuscript (any remaining errors are entirely my own).

Shanelle Webb, Jeff Grant, and Ophelia Nelly May Humphreys-Elvis who all helped by encouraging me to produce this collection and by commenting on my work.

I owe particular thanks to my friend Jeff for his detailed comments on a number of the poems in this book.

I am grateful to OpenAI, (https://openai.com/) for making available a free version of Chat GPT and allowing me to use their model to experiment poetically (for the results of my experimentation, see the section entitled "Poetry and Chat GPT").

How Sweet and Sad was the Bird

How sweet and sad was the bird
I heard
As I stood at my open window.

When I go
To the pub to meet my friends,
We will pretend
That there is no end;
Or at least hide for a while
In the smile
Produced by drink,
Which makes men think
That all
This will last.

But I shall recollect the bird's call
As I stood at my open window
And know
That all
That sings must pass.

Lovers by Moonlight

Lad and lass
Find delight
By moonlight
In spring grass,
Where the breeze
Does tease,
Then pass.

Poet (An Acrostic)

Poetry maybe, for better or worse,
Of the kind we call free verse.
Each muse does her poet choose.
Though some may say that I lie.

Autumn Thoughts

In autumn, I recollect
How I would collect
The autumn fall
From the forest's floor.
How many more
Shall I recall?

A Small Island in a Great Sea

A small island in a great sea.
Once, half the world was painted red
And we engaged in slavery.
It is so often said
That the British Empire did no good.
Yet (having abolished slavery), we patrolled seas
Stopping those who still engaged
In the cruel slave trade.

As I stood
In this remnant
Of the Great
North Wood
I thought on those who hate
This country.

Now our former colonies are free
To have their own mess
(Or progress);
And we
Have the cold sea
And what we
Call progress.

Abandoned

A remembrance of hands
And an abandoned hairband,
Kept for a while,
Brings a sad smile
To a man's ageing face
At a girl's lost grace.

I Have Awoken to Birdsong

I have awoken to birdsong
And lain awake
Until sleep takes me again.
I measure time
With clocks. Birds and flowers
Know not hours,
Nor do they see me
Conversing with time
In a half rhyming rhyme
Until my song is done.

After Death

I pass by graves
On a rain-soaked day.
I know those below
Do not regret the wet.

I relish the fresh
Scents of this passing day
For after my death
I will know
No rain below.

This Little March Snow

This little March snow
Soon must go.
And spring birds sing
Over tombs.

The Churchyard Path

People passed
Me on the churchyard path
That I walk
So oft,
Caught in my passing thoughts,
(Many now forgot).
Then came the rain
To wash all who pass
Along this fleeting path.

My Coffee Grows Cold

My coffee grows cold
And I old.
And here I sit,
Playing the wit,
Until death calls time
On wit
And rhyme.

An Autumn Day

Damp leaves in cold park.
Autumn days are growing dark.
The wind whistled
In the churchyard.
Then the rain came again.

Nature

We may try to deny
That Mother Nature is there.
But the burr
On our clothes,
The prick of the rose,
And twigs in our hair,
Show what we know:
That nature is there.

As I Write

As I write,
Church bells tell
Of dust
And night.

I Always Return

I always return
To the tick tock
Of the clock,
From which I learn
To accept and respect
That I
Will die.

This sunlit day
Must pass away
And I must write
Whilst there is light.

As the Autumn Weather Grows Colder

As the autumn weather grows colder
And I older,
The thought of warm bedclothes
With a Kate
Or a Rose
Still appeals.

I have known heels
That measure
My pleasure.
But pleasure passes
For rakes and lasses
And the graveyard grasses
Claim our name.

Autumn Birds

I heard autumn birds
And did think
Of strong drink.
And felt the fire
Of autumn lust.

Man sates his desire
For sweet forget
In a girl's arms.
For in dust,
All charms
We forget.

An Autumn Morning

In the early morning
Few birds I heard.
In the distance
Vehicles passed by.

On such autumn mornings
I have no resistance
To thoughts of mortality.

But half dark
Turns to light
And I must
Shake off dust.

But autumn
Will come
And leaves fall.

Background

My clock's chime
Is background sound
To my rhyme.

I raise my glass
To old Father Time
Who will outlast
This poor rhyme.

Who Knows

Some thought his poetry meant this
And others that.
He wore a hat
Sometimes
And often (being lost in rhymes)
Went out with no raincoat.

He had no moat
And little private wealth.
The reader sighs
Trying to categorise
The poet's view.
Some declare he was a Tory of the deepest blue
(While others protest this was not true)!

A few saw a man of the left;
But found themselves bereft
On finding verse which, they say,
Romanticised the nobility of yesterday.

Perhaps the poet smiles somewhere.
Or perchance he doesn't care.
For who knows
Where the rhymer goes
When his ink runs dry

And his words finally die.

(Composed on June 4th 2017.)

Brief

Church bells briefly heard.
Something falls
From an autumn tree.
A solitary
Bird momentarily calls,
Maybe to me.

In Early December

In early December
November's leaves still adorn
The woodland lawn.
Man's pattern is made
In light and shade
And the gardener's rake
Rakes all leaves.

Janus

Janus waits in the wings.
As with previous dead years
He will bring
Laughter and tears.

Doors open and close.
The futurologist thinks he knows
What the future holds.

But Janus thumbs his nose,
And history goes
On as before;
And where it goes
Heaven only knows.

A Warning of Dust

I have felt love and lust,
And coughed in the early morning.
A warning
Of dust.

The Morning After

I make tea
While she
Takes a shower.

I know
In an hour
Or so
She will go.

She smokes a cigarette
At my open window.
I regret
The cigarette.

Endings

Soon November
Will become December
And January
Will follow on.
How soon
Another year
Is gone!

A Tree Grows

A tree grows.
Its branches entwining
With another tree,
Forming a canopy
Under which pass
A lad and his lass.

Seasons pass
And saplings grow to maturity,
While the lad and lass
We did see
Forever lie
Under sky and tree.

Secret Giggles

Secret giggles.
Young women's wriggles.
A moment of pleasure
In hot weather.

Civilisation

A lightning flash
The splash
Of urban rain.

The roar
Of Thor
In London Town.

Civilisation goes down
In fire
And rain.

Commuter Train

I sat alone
On a train
In early morning.
When a young woman on her phone
Said, "Are you still with your friend?"

The memory remains.
A couple yawning
In early morning.
And 2 strangers on a commuter train.

Eternity

On my walks,
I often find
That inner talk
Distracts my mind.

Then the breeze
Rustles autumn leaves,
Reminding me
Of eternity.

Fallen Churchyard Leaves

Walking through fallen leaves
In the familiar churchyard,
The poet sees
The hard
Fact that all
Leaves fall.

Fame

Would I be glad to have
This thing called fame?
I think to win the game
Would be good.

But in the wood
Leaves turn brown
On the ground.

Going to Church

I keep meaning to go
To the church I so
Often pass. Its gravestones
Say, "Skin and bone
Must fade away."
So I know
I will go
To church one day.

I Enter the Graveyard

I enter the graveyard
Where men forget regret
While the living
Forget their eternal
Bed is made
In waiting grave

And choose to lose
Their day
In play
With technology,
Which makes none free
Of the eternal grave.

I Heard a Leaf Fall

I heard a leaf fall.
It fell, dry and dead,
And rested there
On greying head.
And brought a thought
Of the passing kind
Into my so mortal mind.

I Heard the Wind Blow

I heard the wind blow
Through this wood I love.
When I go,
Wind will blow.
And rain pour,
Though I am no more.
Yet it comforts me so.

I Recall Honeysuckle on a Wall

I recall honeysuckle on a wall
And the scent of Grandfather's roses.
The poet composes
A rhyme
To Time
Who ends all.

Nesting Boxes

I recall the nesting box
On my grandfather's shed.
Blue Tits laid their eggs.
Some grew and flew
Away.

January seems dead.
Yet, in the churchyard, birds
Sing.

And, come the spring,
Birds will lay in boxes
To the delight
Of young children.
And foxes bark
In the depths of night.

Fairies

In childhood, we play
With fairies. But they
Do not stay
And we engage
On the world's stage.

Then, in old age,
We fancy
We see
A fairy
Ere we enter eternity.

I See Sunlight

I see sunlight
On my bed.
Perchance we dance
In fleeting light,
Then vanish
Into night.

In the Crowded Pub

In the crowded pub,
A teen Goth girl
Sings of forever love.

We cheer over beers
And raise our glass
To a Goth girl

And the truth
That all youth
Must pass.

And all our suns
Must become
The black.

It's Close to 1am When

It's close to 1am when
I hear the wild wind shake
My window. Later, when I go
Out, I will see
How his dances
Have made free
With poor branches
And leaves,
Brought low
By his breeze.

When men go
Among fallen trees
And scattered leaves,
They know they too must go
And join fallen trees and leaves.

My Favourite Room

My favourite room
Is my bedroom.
A quiet place
With a bookcase
Full of books.

And a glass
Where girls look
As they pass
By. And I
Return to books.

On Hearing Birdsong

On hearing birdsong
I am glad
That I am here
To hear
Their sad, glad song.

We die
And our love
Dies with us.

No, it lives on
When we are gone
In those we love.

And the birds
Sing on
With no care
For where
We have gone.

Poetry in Rain

Listening to rain
While reading poetry.
But why read poetry
When there is rain?
For there is poetry
In the rain.

Soon Autumn Will Come

Soon autumn will come
And girl's feet pass
Over leaves and grass.
But the churchyard clock
They will notice not.

Soon the Autumn Moon

Soon the autumn moon
Will come
And autumn's milder face
Will replace
The boiling summer sun.

But the poet sees
Autumn's fallen leaves
Broiled by summer's sun
Long ere autumn
Is due to come.

Drought

Dry leaves hang
On waiting trees.
The dead litter.
The cracked ground.
Our bitter
Harvest of drought.

I am Swallowed by Dark

I am swallowed by dark
In the churchyard at night.
Then a brief gleam of the floodlight
Shows the graves all stark and white.

My feet return to peopled street
And I drink of life's wine,
For I must smile
While I have time.

I Heard the Owl Cry

I heard the owl cry.
The churchyard is close by;
The dead weep not
In their little plot.
Only I heard him cry,
Then found my temporary sleep.

The Wind Sings

The wind sings
In the trees
As I,
Alone,
Pass by
Gravestone.

Or, on the busy thoroughfare,
Oft he catches me unaware
With piles of fallen leaves
And great boughs brought low.
And then I know
That all must go.

There is No Light

There is no light
To brighten the night
As I pass
Along the churchyard path.
Just gusting wind
Eternal as the rain.

My Dog Kicks Earth

My dog kicks earth.
There is sleep.
And death,
Which is the final
Sleep in earth.

My Dog (Still Young)

My dog (still young)
Enjoys these fallen leaves
Flung across pavements
By winter's breeze,
Where they lie
As he and I
Pass by
On a December day.

We Love the Wood

We love the wood
By day
And take our delight
In glades.
But when light fades
And day
Is swallowed by night,
Fears play.

We Fuss and Rush

We fuss
And rush
Through life.
Perhaps take
A lover,
A husband,
Or wife.

We will find time
To weave our rhyme,
We say,
For there must
Be another day.
And the dust
Gathers unseen.

We are Sparks

We are sparks
In the dark.
A brief light
Piercing the night.
But no spark
Conquers the dark.

Winter's Last Blast

Winter's last blast
Sighs and dies
In a rhyme
Of passing springtime.

The Thunder Spoke

The thunder spoke
And I awoke
To heavy rain.
I lay awake
Pondering on lakes
And climate change.

I took pleasure
In rainy weather
As a child
But this wild
Storm warns
Of change.

5 Degrees

5 degrees.
Wet trees
Drip yesterday's rain.
The autumn came
Bringing acorns
And precious rain
To woodland lawns.

There is Deep Mud

There is deep mud
In the park again.
As I wade through flood,
I sigh
And cudgel my poor brain
To explain
Why we poets romanticise
This thing called rain!

There is Part of the Park

There is part
Of the park,
Mysterious and dark,
Where wind sings
Always to me.
And I
Am free.

We 2 Took a Short Cut Through

We 2 took a shortcut through
The place of stones and bones.
I have some time to rhyme
Of a young woman who
May read this one day
And, pondering on weathered old gravestones,
Say, "We are but clay."

While there is Time

All this must pass away.
Yet there is still time
To rhyme
Of nymphs in short dresses
Who play
In glades
Of the poet's fertile mind.

Work Meeting

As the meeting neared its end,
My old friend,
Who had not
Yet said a word
(Leastways, I heard
Him not),
Interrupted and did say,
"Tick tock."
Yet the clock
Is forever ticking away
Our day,
Though oft we heed him not.

A Summer Butterfly

A butterfly
On a
Sunny day
Flew by
My Labrador.
A snap of jaw
And our summer chat
Of this and that.

All things must die
As the summer butterfly.
Death's jaws will close
On man and rose.
You and I
Are but butterflies
Who love and laugh
And then must pass.

An Ordinary Saturday

On my way
To eat breakfast
In a café
On an ordinary
Saturday, I heard birds.
While in Ukraine's Kiev
Birdsong was drowned
Out by bombs.

(I stand with Ukraine)

An Old Clock Chimes

As an old clock chimes,
An ageing poet rhymes
Of girls in summer frocks
Who think not on clocks.
But old Father Time
He ends all rhyme.

As the Light Slowly Dimmed

As the light
Slowly dimmed
I took delight
In birds.
"Oh my god!"
But words
Are not birds.

Birds in the Early Morning

When, at 6am, I
Walked in the woods nearby,
Expecting to hear the birds
(As I have often heard
Them sing in early morn).
Few birds I heard
For as I slept
The dawn
She crept
Softly by.

Words

I hear the birds
And think on windblown
Words out flown
By birds.

Caught in Useless Thought

Caught in useless thought
On a sunny day,
I entered that place
Of light and shade.
That unknown space
Where we
Are made
To face
Our own mortality.

Fallen Blossom

I found
Blossom on the ground;
Which brought
To mind the thought,
We all,
As the blossom, fall.

Flowers in Springtime

Flowers in springtime
Bring to mind
A former springtime.
But I find
That my November
And oncoming December
Haunts my mind.

I Get Up in the Dark

I get up in the dark
And start
My day.
And when my sky grows dark
Some may say, "He left art,
Then his day
Closed in dark."

I Start to Write

I start
To write
As morning's light
Begins to show.
The dark
Must follow
Morning's glow.
Only the hollow
Do not know
That tis so.

In an English Garden

In an English garden,
I heard a blackbird
And thought on England;
And on how we
English are still,
More or less,
Free.

Young Women's Feet

Young women's feet
Kick autumn leaves.
Time deceives
Not. Clocks
Do stop.
And once-green leaves
Must turn to dust.

Outside

Birds outside my window
Visit me today.
But they
Never stay.

Young women go
By on the street.
Their stilettoed feet
Tick tock like clocks.

And I rhyme
Of old Father Time
And clocks
That stop.

Just Dust

I find my scalp flaking.
Bits of dead skin escaping.
But they are not me
For I am sweet poetry.
Yet my little sun
Shall one day become
Just dust.

On Hearing Crows

On hearing crows
Macbeth and death
Fill my mind.
Though death goes
In many clothes.
Still I find
That black crows
Peck my mind.

Progress

As for me
I do not agree
With the inevitability
Of progress. Good poetry
And friends
Are ends
In themselves.
Give me
Oak bookshelves
Laden with treasures.
These are the pleasures
I would have
To make me glad.

As I Progress

Walking through the churchyard
On a freezing evening,
I consider progress
And pass by
Fading inscriptions
On tombstones.

Playing Around in Cyberspace

Playing around in cyberspace
We come face-to-face
With the vanity
And utter banality
Of our flawed humanity.

Scrolling

In constant scrolling
We find Gradgrind,
Doling
Out the same
Diet
Of pleasure and pain
To the unquiet mind.

They Talk of All-Powerful AI

They talk of all-powerful AI.
Perhaps this is Sci-Fi.
Or maybe it is true.
But you and I
Will surely die,
Unless we
Achieve immortality
And perhaps live on
After the body is gone
In virtual reality.
But would that be
You and I?

A Transhumanist Heard a Clock Tick

A Transhumanist heard a clock tick
And said, "Time I shall lick!"
And the Clock said, "Progress,
Regress, progress, regress"
As the clock's hands did trace
The clock's round face,
From beginning to beginning,
Forever spinning:
"Progress, regress,
Progress, regress."
And the Transhumanist said
Nought, for he was long since dead.

Corporate Types

Corporate types programme likes
Into computers
Where they are heard
By commuters;
And a middle-aged poet
Who romanticises vinyl
And exchanges a final word
With the barmaid,
Who doesn't remember vinyl.

Me, on the Periphery

Me, on the periphery,
Engaging in desultory
Conversation with the barman.
As they sing karaoke.

I say goodnight
To the lone barman.
Momentarily partake
Of the firelight,
Then forsake
It for the night.

Shadows of the Past

My shadow in front of me.
Leaves fall from a nearby tree.
I think of an old England
I never knew.

Is all I understand,
Or maybe half-see,
The reality of me?

What is true
When the many/few
Call for Britain's statues to fall
And label me merely a reactionary?

Jubilee

A moderate patriotism is good
And I raise a glass
To my queen and country.
While, in the ancient wood,
The eternal wind does pass
Over tree
And grass.

The Inadequacy of Verse

I heard a Blackbird
And did curse
The inadequacy of verse.
He knows not poetry,
Yet outdoes me
In verse.

Poetry and Chat GPT

Note

The first poem in this section "All Love and Lust" was composed with the assistance of Chat GPT, software developed by OpenAI (https://openai.com/).

The software composed a poem, following my prompt to write a poem beginning "All love and lust ends in dust". I then modified the poem composed by Chat GPT to produce my own (much shorter) version, which draws heavily on that written by the AI software.

The second poem, "My Old Clock I Wind", is my own work and is reproduced here in full. I then asked Chat GPT to compose a poem using the first two lines of "My Old Clock I Wind". Chat GPT's reworking of my poem appears below the original.

The third poem in this section, "Midnight", was wholly composed by me and is reproduced in full. It is then followed by Chat GPT's continuation of my poem.

I am grateful to OpenAI for making a free version of Chat GPT available for interested users to experiment with.

My Poem "All Love and Lust" and Chat GPT

"All Love and Lust" as Composed by Chat GPT

Continue this poem: all love and lust ends in dust

All love and lust, like fleeting gusts, May lift us high, but then they must Descend to earth, to join the rust And crumble into grains of dust.

Though passion's fire may burn so bright, It's but a spark in endless night, And soon it fades, like dying light, To leave us empty, void of sight.

For all that's born will surely die, And all that lives must say goodbye. No matter how we try and try, We're bound to fall, to fade, to lie.

So let us love with open hearts, And let us cherish every part Of those we hold, before we depart And join the cycle, where we start.

For though all love and lust ends in dust, It's in the moment, in the trust, That we find joy, that we find lust, That we find life, before we're thrust Into the endless, timeless gust That leaves us naught but grains of dust.

"All Love and Lust" as Rewritten by Kevin Morris

Though passion's fire may burn so bright,
It's but a spark in endless night,
And soon it fades, like dying light,
To leave us lost to human sight.

For all that's born will surely die
And you and I must say goodbye.
No man can the great leveller deny
And dust must take both you and I.

My Poem "My Old Clock I wind" and Chat GPT

"My Old Clock I Wind" as Composed by Kevin Morris

My old clock I wind
And much philosophy therein find.
I can bring
The pendulum's swing
To a stop with my hand;
Yet I cannot command
Time to default
On his duty and halt
The passing of the years.
He has no ears
For our laughter and tears
And his sickle will swing on
Long after we are gone.

"My Old Clock I Wind" as Rewritten by Chat GPT

Write a poem beginning "my old clock I wind and much philosophy therein find"

My old clock I wind and much philosophy therein find, With each passing tick, a thought comes to mind, As the hands move forward, I feel time slipping away, The moments I hold dear, a memory in delay.

The clock's steady rhythm, a constant reminder, That life is but fleeting, a transient confider, Of dreams left behind and moments to cherish, Each second a gift, a memory to relish.

The clock ticks on, unwavering and sure, Reminding me of moments that will endure, Of loves lost and friends departed, Of memories to be cherished, not to be outsmarted.

So I wind my old clock, and with each turn, I'm reminded of life's fleeting concern, Of the moments to come, and those that have passed, And I cherish each tick, for they never last.

My Poem "Midnight" and Chat GPT

"Midnight" as Composed by Kevin Morris

Midnight, black as pitch. No scheming demon, ghost, nor witch. Only the darkness, which in the human heart resides, manifests itself in cruelty and pride.

"Midnight" as Continued by Chat GPT

Midnight, black as pitch. No scheming demon, ghost, nor witch. Only the darkness, which in the human heart resides, manifests itself in cruelty and pride.

Yet in the shadows of this midnight hour, Lies a glimmer of hope, a guiding power. A light that shines, dispelling all fear, Bringing comfort, banishing the tear.

For in the heart of every man and woman, Lies a spark of love, a gentle flame, burning. A force that fights against the night, Bringing peace and hope, making everything right.

So though midnight may seem bleak and grim, Let us not forget, it's just a passing phase. For with the dawn comes a brand new day, And a chance to make a brighter way.

The Poet

I confess,
I undress
Women in my mind.
Some are true lovers
While others
I find
Are the temporary kind.

And my love and lust
Are dust.
Poets die
And leave behind
A part
Of their heart
And mind.

And readers discuss
The loves and lusts
We leave behind,
Be they real
Or the imagined kind.

Contact and Social Media

To contact Kevin, please send an email to kmorrispoet@gmail.com.

Website: https://kmorrispoet.com/

Twitter: https://twitter.com/drewdog2060_

Instagram: https://www.instagram.com/kmorrispoet/

Printed in Great Britain
by Amazon

20779874R00068